A Wee Scottish Cookbook

Cristine Eastin

Published by Cristine Eastin, 2018.

A Wee Scottish Cookbook
Copyright © 2018 by Cristine Eastin
Cover design by Jason Pape, Papesite Creative, LLC
Photo tartan background © Ruth Black/Shutterstock
Photo Scottish landscape © Freddie Marriage/Unsplash
Print ISBN-13: 978-0-9994827-3-5
ISBN-10: 0-9994827-3-4
eBook ISBN-13: 978-0-9994827-4-2
ISBN-10: 0-9994827-4-2
Published by Cristine Eastin
Visit the author's website: CristineEastin.com[1]

CONTENTS

INTRODUCTION

Eating my way around Scotland has been a delicious adventure. So when wrote the first book in the series *A Highland Romance*, the characters had to eat some of my favorite foods. As a result, readers got hungry and asked for recipes.

Here, then, in this little companion cookbook, are twenty recipes inspired by my novel *Love Inherited*.

Food is a thick slice of the Scottish culture in *Love Inherited*, and when China MacLeish, an American turned reluctant heiress, finds herself dropped in to the seaside village of Fionnloch and into Sylvie Blair's kitchen, culture shock at being offered blood sausage for breakfast almost causes her to dribble coffee down her sweater front. But Sylvie serves up love to heal a wounded heart with every dish she cooks and every cup of tea she pours.

I love Scotland and I love writing about Scotland. My desire is that reader step into the tartan world of marrow-chilling mists and purple-clad hills, of no nonsense Highlanders who offer a smile and a dram—that they smell the arom of venison stew simmering on the old Aga cooker, savor shortbread that crumbles over the tongue—and imagine they are there.

Join me on this tasting tour of the Highlands of Scotland.

The ingredients in *A Wee Scottish Cookbook* are given in US and UK measurements to keep cooks on either side of the pond from pulling their hair out You, the cook, don't have to remember that the UK pint is 20 ounces, while the US pint is 16 ounces—and other differences that are enough to make a cook book writer's brain explode. When it comes to tablespoons and fractions thereof, note that the UK tablespoon is equivalent to 1.2 US tablespoons. Mostly I didn't translate tablespoon measurements, as precision isn't critical in man recipes. And I rounded centigrade oven temps a bit.

Converting flour from US cups to grams is another tangle of numbers. here's quite a bit of difference in weight between types of flour, manufacturers f flour, and scales to weigh the flour. I use the conversion chart at King Arthur our[1].

A few handy cook's tools I recommend in recipe directions are: an immer- on blender, a coffee grinder, and parchment paper. Immersion blenders make uréed soup a snap. No more messy transferring batches to a blender. Speaking f messes, grinding my own coffee got to be a chore, so now I use the grinder for ains, nuts, and spices. Clean the grinder by pulsing 2 tablespoons of rice to fine owder, then brush out the grinder and lid. Parchment paper is another mess- ver. Line a baking tray with parchment paper for nonstick baking, even brown- g, and quick clean up. Look for it on the grocery shelf with aluminum foil and astic wrap.

And lastly, cooking is both science and art. Owing to variances in actual oven mperatures, style of cooking—or simply your preferences—you may find or eate some differences to what I've set down here. I welcome your comments. ontact me through my website at CristineEastin.com[2].

. https://www.kingarthurflour.com/learn/ingredient-weight-chart.html

. http://cristineeastin.com

PORRIDGE

Stick-to-your-ribs porridge is as quintessentially Scottish as haggis. And i might also work for wallpaper paste. I'm talking about long-cooking steel cu oats, not quick rolled oats that Americans call oatmeal. Highly underrated an taken for granted, porridge is good for you; it's allegedly a natural cholester scrubber. I can't say that it's lowered my cholesterol, but my daily bowl of po ridge—topped with brown sugar, fresh fruit, and yogurt—makes me happy, s maybe it lowers my blood pressure.

Carrbridge, Scotland is home to the annual World Porridge Making Cham pionship, where the winner claims the Golden Spurtle award. A spurtle is a spe cial wooden stick to stir the porridge. Looking a little like a wand, a spurtle mus cast a spell on the porridge, otherwise I can't think why a spoon doesn't wor just as well. When I stayed for a night in the picturesque village of Carrbridge, hoped to find a spurtle with which to stir my porridge, but I came away spurtle less.

If you want to go wild with porridge recipes, find them at the Golden Spur tle[1] website.

But for a basic porridge recipe, read on.

INGREDIENTS

1 cup (200g) steel cut (pinhead) oats

3 cups (708ml) water

Salt to taste

DIRECTIONS

Bring salted water to boil.

Add oats and stir.

Cover and simmer for 30-35 minutes, stirring occasionally.

---

1.   https://goldenspurtle.com/recipes/

NOTES: Set the pot lid cockeyed a bit to let steam out to prevent boiling over. I made a mess of my stovetop many times before I learned this tip. Works for rice too.

Don't be alarmed if a greenish tinge appears on top of the oats while cooking. From what I've read, this is due to a chemical reaction to something in the water and is harmless. Just stir it in.

For a treat, add a dollop of the caramel sauce that goes with the Sticky Toffee Pudding recipe.

I cook up a triple batch of porridge and freeze it. Sometimes I throw in raisins or dried cranberries so the fruit is cooked nice and tender. And porridge is good as leftovers. As Sylvie says in *Love Inherited*, "Yesterday's porridge is as good today. And it's quick."

SCOTCH BROTH

S ylvie cooks up a pot of Scotch Broth in her little cottage in *Love Inherited*. I don't know if Sylvie makes her Scotch Broth with the traditional lamb meat, but I do know that Granny Nan says Sylvie's soup needs "mair pepper."

Variations of this hearty soup are as individual as the cook and what's in the fridge. Make it on the stovetop, in a crock pot, or in a kettle hanging from a pot crane over a hearth fire. Make it thicker or thinner. I make it with stewing beef.

Be sure and add the secret ingredient: time. Scotch Broth shouldn't be hurried. Much like a trip to the Highlands.

INGREDIENTS
2 tablespoons butter or oil
1 medium onion, diced
3 cloves garlic, minced
1-1½ pounds (454-700g) stewing beef, cubed
½ cup (107g) medium pearled barley
⅓ cup (75g) dried green split peas
6 cups (48 ounces) low-sodium chicken broth
1 teaspoon salt
fresh ground pepper to taste
2-4 bay leaves
4 sprigs thyme or 1-1½ teaspoons dried thyme
1 large carrot, diced
1 turnip, peeled and diced
1 small rutabaga (swede/neep), peeled and diced
1 parsnip, peeled and diced
2 sticks celery, diced
1 medium leek, white and green parts, chopped and rinsed
a leaf or two chopped kale

DIRECTIONS

Crock Pot

Toss all ingredients in a crock pot and cook on Low 9-10 hours.

Stovetop

In a Dutch oven or large soup pot, sauté onions and garlic in butter or oil until tender, adding garlic the last couple minutes.

Add beef, barley, split peas, broth, salt, pepper, bay leaves, and thyme. Bring to a boil, reduce heat. Cover and simmer 2 hours.

Add carrot, turnip, rutabaga, parsnip, and celery. Simmer another hour.

Remove bay leaves and thyme sprigs.

Add leek and kale. Simmer 30 minutes more.

NOTES: On a blistering summer day in Wisconsin, I made Scotch Broth. I couldn't bear to heat up the house, so I let the soup simmer in a crock pot for 10 hours overnight. The result was a thick, mild-flavored soup with a wonderful texture due to the barley and split peas. But I agreed with Granny Nan, it needed mair pepper."

Add any root vegetable, dried bean, or meat (or no meat at all) to your Scotch Broth.

This recipe makes a lot of soup; invite the neighbors over.

Adapted from recipe at The Daring Gourmet[1].

---

1. https://www.daringgourmet.com/traditional-scotch-broth/

SWEET PEA CREAM SOUP

Sweet Pea Cream Soup is not your winter-warmer split pea soup: it's a garden fresh tasting creamy soup that's good hot or cold. And it's such a pretty shade of green.

In *Love Inherited*, China MacLeish enjoys Sweet Pea Cream Soup at the Blade and Bear with Duncan Sinclair, *Laird of Fionnloch. Is it a date? Or is it just dinner out with a friend?

INGREDIENTS

4 tablespoons butter (57g)

1 medium onion, chopped

1 leek, white and light green parts, chopped and rinsed

2 cloves garlic, minced

1 heaping tablespoon all-purpose (plain) flour

4 cups (32 ounces) low-sodium chicken broth

2 packages frozen baby or petite peas (10 ounces each), thawed, or fresh shelled peas (about 5 cups)

½ cup (15g) fresh mint leaves, chopped

1 cup (236ml) whipping cream (double cream)

salt and cracked black pepper to taste

optional—1-2 tablespoons lemon juice

DIRECTIONS

In a large soup pot or Dutch oven, melt butter and sauté leek and onion about 5 minutes.

Add garlic and sauté 1 minute longer.

Add flour and stir to coat onion and leek.

Add chicken broth, slowly stirring in.

Add peas and simmer until tender, about 3 minutes for frozen and 5 minutes for fresh.

Remove pot from heat.

Stir in mint and cream.

Purée soup with immersion blender, or purée in batches using regular ender.

Return pot to low heat. Add salt and pepper and lemon juice, if desired. ook gently 5-10 minutes. Do not boil.

Serve hot or chilled. Garnish with dollop of crème fraîche or sour cream. orinkle with chopped chives or mint.

NOTES: I highly recommend investing in a good immersion blender.

In my opinion, about 1½ tablespoons lemon juice gives the right zip.

*A laird is the owner of a large and long-established estate in Scotland. *Laird* a description, not a title, dating to the fifteenth century, though many holders the designation may have hereditary and conferred titles as well. In *Love Inher-ed*, readers meet Sir Duncan Eideard Armstrong Sinclair, 10th Baronet, Laird Fionnloch, owner of Glengorm House and the surrounding 65,000-acre estate the western Highlands of Scotland.

Adapted from recipe by Ina Garten[1].

https://www.foodnetwork.com/recipes/ina-garten/fresh-pea-soup-recipe-1937479

CULLEN SKINK

Though the name sounds a little suspect, like it's made from a small High-land rodent or smelly fungus, Cullen skink simply means soup from Cullen, a town on the northeast coast of Scotland.

The Bridge Inn at Ratho, just south of Edinburgh Airport, serves up incred-bly tasty Cullen Skink.

This soup doesn't appear in *Love Inherited*, but I like it so much, some char-acter in a future book in the series will dine on Cullen Skink.

INGREDIENTS

1 pound (½kg) smoked haddock or any undyed smoked fish

2 cups (470ml) whole (homogenized) milk

6 tablespoons (85g) butter

2 large leeks, white and light green parts, chopped and rinsed

2 medium onions, finely chopped

2 cloves garlic, crushed

2 medium potatoes, peeled and diced

2 cups (470ml) half and half (single cream)

1 cup (236ml) whipping cream (double cream)

Salt and white pepper to taste

2-3 tablespoons dry white wine

Parsley and chives, chopped, to garnish

DIRECTIONS

In a large saucepan, poach fish in milk, placing fish skin-side down in singl layer. Do not boil milk. Poach, simmering 8-10 minutes or until fish is opaqu Turn halfway through to skin-side up.

With a slotted spoon, transfer fish to a plate, reserving milk. When the fis has cooled a bit, remove skin and flake fish with your fingers, removing all bone

While fish is cooling, melt butter in Dutch oven or soup pot and sauté onions and leeks until tender and translucent, about 10 minutes. Add garlic last 2 minutes.

Pour reserved milk into pot. Add potatoes. Add half and half and bring to simmer. Stir frequently until potatoes are tender, about 30-40 minutes.

Roughly mash vegetables, leaving chunks of potatoes.

Add flaked fish.

Add whipping cream and white wine and heat to hot but not bubbling. Salt and pepper to taste.

Serve garnished with chopped parsley and chives.

Adapted from recipe by Ben Watson[1], Head Chef at the Bridge Inn at Ratho.

1.   http://www.heraldscotland.com/life_style/14371949.Recipe_of_the_Day__Cullen_Skink/

STEAK AND ALE PIE

C hina MacLeish takes off for the local pub, the Anchor Inn, when she's desperate to escape her house guest. Steak and Ale Pie is an Anchor specialty.

Steak and Ale Pie belongs in the comfort food category as far as I'm concerned—like beef stew only better. It's a rustic dish that looks great in a stoneware deep dish pie plate or cast iron skillet with the corners of the puff pastry drooping over the edge.

INGREDIENTS

2 pounds (1kg) chuck roast steak, cut into 1-1½-inch cubes

¼ cup (30g) all-purpose (plain) flour

3 tablespoons vegetable oil

1 cup (142g) sliced onions

4 ounces (113g) diced pancetta

1-3 cloves garlic, minced (more garlic is better)

12-ounce bottle (355ml) dark ale, stout, or porter beer, divided

4 tablespoons (60ml) Worcestershire sauce

2 tablespoons tomato paste

1 tablespoon (14g) sugar

1 tablespoon fresh rosemary, finely chopped

1 tablespoon fresh sage, chopped

1 cup (236ml) beef broth

½ teaspoon salt

¼ teaspoon cracked black pepper

8 ounces (227g) mushrooms, halved or quartered if large

1 tablespoon cornstarch (cornflour)

1 tablespoon water

1 egg, beaten

1 sheet frozen puff pastry, thawed but chilled

DIRECTIONS
Preheat oven to 325°F (165°C, Gas Mark 3).
Dredge beef in flour in a bowl until evenly coated.
Brown half the beef in half the oil in Dutch oven over high heat until edges re crispy. Transfer to a bowl or plate. Brown remaining beef and add to the rest.
Sauté onion and pancetta in remaining oil over medium heat. Cook until nion medium tender. Add garlic last 2 minutes.
Add half cup beer and deglaze pan, scraping up the good bits in the pan. Simler 2 minutes.
Turn off heat.
Add Worcestershire sauce, tomato paste, sugar, and herbs. Stir.
Add remaining 1 cup beer and beef broth. Salt and pepper to taste.
Mix in mushrooms and browned beef. Stir to combine. Transfer to deep dish ie plate.
Cover with foil. Bake 2 hours.
Uncover and bake 30 minutes more.
Remove pie from oven.
Increase oven temperature to 400°F (205°C, Gas Mark 6).
Dissolve cornstarch with water. Add hot broth to cornstarch mixture a little t a time to thin. Stir into pie filling.
Unfold pastry, forming a square. Lift pastry onto the pie. Brush with beaten gg.
Bake pie another 30 minutes or until pastry is dark gold and nicely puffed.
Let pie rest a few minutes and eat.
NOTES: The dish I use is an old crockery deep dish with 3-inch sides. It's erfect for this Steak and Ale pie.
Pancetta is Italian bacon; if you can't find it, thick-sliced bacon, diced, works.
The choice of ale will affect the complexity of the flavor; I used a Scotch ale. 1y husband gave this recipe a big thumbs up. Between mouthfuls, he said, "Re-ember that steak and ale pie we had on Skye? This is better."
Adapted from recipe at Foodness Gracious[1].

---

1. https://foodnessgracious.com/steak-ale-pie/

HEARTY VENISON STEW

Craggan Mhor, the manor house China MacLeish inherits, is a Highland hunting lodge, so venison would surely be on the menu for dinner—slow cooked in the Aga's simmering oven. The meaty aroma reaches down the long tartan-carpeted hall, hung with old claymores and brass-studded leather shields, to the great oak front door.

Scottish red deer stags are impressive animals. While staying at Glengarry Castle Hotel, my husband and I watched two stags approach each other on a ridge on the other side of Loch Oich, roaring as they marched to a fight they decided not to have.

INGREDIENTS

1 pound (½kg) stewing venison, cut into 1-inch cubes

¼ cup (30g) all-purpose (plain) flour, divided

2 tablespoons olive oil

1 onion, chopped

3 celery stalks, sliced on the diagonal

2 carrots, sliced

4 ounces (113g) portabella mushrooms, quartered

1-4 cloves garlic, crushed

1¼ cups (300ml) dry red wine

1 scant cup (200ml) low-sodium beef stock

½ teaspoon allspice (or cinnamon, cloves, and nutmeg mixed)

1 tablespoon red currant jelly

1-3 bay leaves

Salt and black pepper to taste

DIRECTIONS

Dredge meat in half flour.

Heat oil in Dutch oven. Add venison. Brown over high heat 5 minutes.

Remove venison, set aside.

Sauté onions, celery, and carrots 3 minutes.

Add mushrooms and garlic, sauté 2 minutes more.

Add remaining flour. Stir to coat vegetables, adding more butter or oil if dry.

Combine red wine and beef stock and gradually blend into mixture. Bring to oil, stirring until thickened, deglazing pot as you stir.

Add allspice, salt and pepper, and red currant jelly. Stir until jelly dissolved. dd bay leaf.

Add venison back in.

Either turn into a crock pot and cook on High 3 hours, or cover with foil or ght lid and cook in oven at 325°F (165°C, Gas Mark 3) 2½-3 hours.

Thicken gravy as desired to finish.

NOTES: I tested Hearty Venison Stew on a way-too-hot day for the oven, so used the crock pot and plugged it in on the screened porch. Normally when I ook in a crock pot, I just dump all the ingredients in, set it on Low, and ignore it r 8-10 hours. Not this time. I went through all the steps as written, and I think e end result was better for it. The vegetables weren't overcooked, and the meat as tender but didn't fall apart. The gravy needed just a bit of thickening at the d.

Adapted from recipe at Recipes at Riverford[1].

. https://www.riverford.co.uk/recipes/view/recipe/venison-red-wine-casserole

SUE'S FISH PIE

My friend Sue says she makes up her fish pie as she goes along—the mark of a true cook, I think. Fish pie is on my list of culinary requests every time visit Sue in Merrie Olde England.

Fish pie is also a common dish in Scotland. One of the things I love about Scotland is that I'm never far from a body of water. And fish are plentiful. But don't just drop a line in any river you happen upon. The fishing rights are owned by the landowner, to whom you must shell out numerous Bank of Scotland notes.

INGREDIENTS

Pie filling

1½ pounds (⅔kg) cod or haddock fillet or mixture of 1 pound white fish and 8 ounces salmon or smoked fish

Handful of cooked shrimp (prawns), peeled

1¾ cups (400ml) milk

2 or 3 hard boiled eggs, roughly chopped

White Sauce

3 tablespoons (40g) butter

¼ cup (30g) all-purpose (plain) flour

Salt, pepper, mustard, lemon juice to taste

Mashed Potato Topping

2 pounds (1kg) Russet (floury) potatoes, peeled, diced, boiled, drained, and mashed with 6 tablespoons (84g) butter, ½-1 teaspoon salt, and 1-2 tablespoon milk

DIRECTIONS

Poach fish in a saucepan with milk and a little salt and pepper. Bring to a boil reduce heat and simmer 5 minutes. Careful not to overcook.

With a slotted spoon, transfer fish to a 9-inch square (or larger) ovenproof dish. Flake fish, removing all bones. Reserve milk. Add shrimp and eggs, distributing evenly over fish.

Make a white sauce with butter, flour, and the milk the fish was cooked in. Pour over fish.

Top with mashed potatoes, spreading all the way to edges of dish so sauce doesn't bubble over. Poke up the mash with a fork to get nice crispy brown peaks. Place dish on a baking tray and bake in oven at 375°F (190°C, Gas Mark 5) 20-40 minutes or until hot. Optional—sprinkle top with shredded cheddar cheese and brown under broiler (grill) 5 minutes.

NOTES: Add anything you like to the sauce. Chopped parsley or chives. Curry paste. Add shredded cheddar cheese to the mashed potatoes.

Use a Scandinavian birch twig whisk for almost foolproof lump-free white sauce.

CHICKEN BONNIE PRINCE CHARLIE

C hicken Bonnie Prince Charlie is an old recipe reportedly gifted to clan MacKinnon as thanks for their assistance to Prince Charlie in his flight to the Isle of Skye after the Battle of Culloden. The true origin of the recipe may be lost in the mist shrouding Skye's rugged mountains, but nevertheless, what has come down to us over the centuries may be the most richly-flavored chicken entrée I've ever tasted.

Drambuie, a liqueur made from Scotch, honey, herbs, and spices, adds a special flavor to this dish. Don't be shy with it; the alcohol cooks out. The melding of simple flavors—Drambuie, cream, butter, apples, and almonds—*mmm, mmm!*

INGREDIENTS

4 chicken breasts, boneless and skinless, cut into strips

Flour, salt, and pepper

6 tablespoons (85g) unsalted butter, divided

5 tablespoons Drambuie (75ml), divided

½ cup (118ml) low-sodium chicken broth

4 apples, peel if skin tough

1 cup (236ml) whipping cream (double cream)

cornstarch (cornflour) to thicken sauce if needed

¼ cup (30g) toasted slivered (flaked) almonds

DIRECTIONS

Place enough flour in a pan or bowl to dredge chicken breasts, stir in salt and pepper. Dredge chicken in the mixture. Shake off excess flour.

Melt half the butter in frying pan or Dutch oven and brown chicken breasts. Douse with half the Drambuie.

Add chicken broth.

Cover and simmer 10 minutes or until done.

Meanwhile, peel and core apples (or leave some peel on for color). Cut into thick slices.

In another frying pan, sauté apple slices in remaining butter until soft.

Remove chicken to 1½-2-inch deep serving dish and keep warm in the oven while making sauce.

To make the sauce, add remaining Drambuie to chicken stock in pan and stir in cream. Heat, but do not boil. Have a little cornstarch mixed in stock or milk ready on the side in case the sauce needs thickening.

Cover chicken with cream sauce, reserving enough sauce to pour over side dishes. Garnish with apple slices and sprinkle with slivered almonds.

Serve with rice and a vegetable.

Adapted from recipe at Rampant Scotland[1].

http://www.rampantscotland.com/recipes/blrecipe_chickenbonnie.htm

VEGETARIAN HAGGIS

Here's the truth about haggis. You cannot stalk a haggis. It's not an elusive wild Highland animal with legs shorter on one side to facilitate running around the hills. It's food—mostly.

Theories abound as to the origin of the dish, from that it dates to ancient Roman times, to that Highland cattle drovers cooked it over campfires. The word haggis is thought to derive from the Old Norse word *haggw*, meaning to hew or strike, reflecting the chopped contents that make up haggis. Regardless, haggis is linked to Scotland like steak and kidney pie is to England.

Before I ordered haggis at the Stein Inn on the Isle of Skye, I asked the server "Sooo, what's really in haggis?" With a straight face he responded: "Oh...oatmeal and sheep bits." I decided to just try it. And I was glad I did.

The "sheep bits" are the liver, heart and lungs, or "sheep's pluck" as the parts are referred to collectively. Not ingredients I would normally choose to eat. In fact, in the US you can't. The Food and Drug Administration has a ban on the import of sheep bits they deem inedible, which would be the lungs. I'm sure that was the fibrous bit I encountered when eating haggis in Inverness, but I tried not to think about it and plowed on through my delicious meal. So you'll have to go to Scotland to eat traditional haggis—or get a sanitized US version.

The other offal truth about traditional haggis that makes the squeamish quail is that, yes indeed, it's boiled in a sheep's stomach. However these days, most commercial haggis is made in a synthetic casing. And anyway, if you order haggis in a restaurant in Scotland, it's usually served scooped out and alongside neeps and tatties—or in a pasty like I had at the Blair Castle cafeteria. My favorite serving presentation is a stack: tatties on the bottom, neeps in the middle, topped with a lightly crisped patty of haggis, and whisky sauce on the side.

Make you want to try it?

Here's a vegetarian dish resembling haggis.

INGREDIENTS

1-2 tablespoons olive oil

1 medium onion, finely chopped

2-3 cloves garlic, minced

1 carrot, finely chopped

1 cup (100g) fresh mushrooms, chopped

3 cups (708ml) vegetable broth

1 cup (200g) steel cut (pinhead) oats

⅓ cup (67g) dry red lentils

¼ cup (55g) canned kidney beans, drained, rinsed, mashed

3-4 tablespoons ground unsalted peanuts

2-3 tablespoons ground hazelnuts

1 tablespoon low-sodium soy sauce

1 tablespoon lemon juice

1½ teaspoons dried thyme

1 teaspoon dried rosemary

1½ teaspoons mixed spice (see *NOTES*)

1 egg, beaten, room temperature

DIRECTIONS

Lightly grease or oil loaf pan 9x5x3 inches (23x13x8 cm).

In a Dutch oven, heat oil and sauté onions over medium heat until tender.

Add garlic and sauté another minute or two.

Add carrots and mushrooms and continue cooking 5 minutes.

Stir in broth, oats, lentils, kidney beans, nuts, soy sauce, lemon juice, and rbs and spices. Bring to a boil, reduce heat. Cover and simmer 30-35 minutes. ir occasionally and check to see if need to add more broth or water.

Preheat oven to 375°F (190°C, Gas Mark 5).

Temper the egg (see *NOTES*) with a little hot broth or water. Stir tempered g into mixture and transfer to baking pan.

Bake 40-60 minutes or until set.

NOTES: To grind nuts, use a food processor or coffee grinder.

Substitute any unsalted nuts.

I prefer fresh chopped rosemary which I grow year-round, keeping it in a pot er the winter on my kitchen counter. Use more if using fresh herbs.

"Mixed spice" can be anything you like: allspice, mace, cinnamon, nutmeg, cloves, ginger, and cayenne.

Tempering the egg is very important, or you'll have scrambled egg. Slowly pour hot liquid into beaten egg, whisking continuously, until egg is brought up to the hotter temperature. Always start with room temperature eggs.

Next time I make Vegetarian Haggis, I'll use a pan that isn't as deep to cut down on the baking time. And because I like more of the slightly crispy top.

I recommend that you go heavy on the garlic, herbs, and spices. Vegetarian Haggis is a satisfying dish that works well as a vegetarian main or as a side.

Adapted from recipe at Allrecipes[1].

1.　　　https://www.allrecipes.com/recipe/81466/vegetarian-haggis/

NEEPS AND TATTIES

Neeps are the same orange-fleshed root vegetable by three names in three generally English-speaking countries: neeps in Scotland, swede in England, and rutabaga in the US. The best explanation for this discrepancy that I can glean is that swede comes from a shortened version of Swedish turnip; rutabaga comes from the Swedish word *rotabagga*, meaning "root bag." And neeps? Short for turnips, one would think. But no, the smaller white turnip isn't a neep. Maybe it's neeps because when winters were harsh in Scotland, farmers fed piles of neeps to their sheeps.

Tatties are potatoes—pronounced like *patties*.

Peel the neep. Slice, dice, and simmer until tender, just like potatoes.

Probably no cook reading this cookbook needs a recipe for mashed potatoes, but I will say that it's a tradition at our house to mash the spuds with the skins on, the resulting mash being called Garbage Potatoes.

Mash both vegetables with your preference of milk, cream, butter, sour cream, and cream cheese.

Neeps and tatties can be mashed and served separately, or mash them together. Top with chopped chives.

RUMBLEDETHUMPS

Included in this wee cookbook because it's Scottish and because the name tickles me and I like saying it. *Rumbledethumps*. It's the Scottish equivalent to Bubble and Squeak in England and Colcannon in Ireland. And it's good.

Use the leftover neeps and tatties from your haggis dinner to make Rumbledethumps. Or make as follows.

INGREDIENTS

4 medium potatoes, peeled and diced

1 medium rutabaga (swede/neep), peeled and diced

⅓-½ cup (75-118ml) milk, heated

4 tablespoons (56g) butter, divided

4 cups (400g) green cabbage, finely shredded

1 medium onion, minced

1 cup (113g) sharp Cheddar cheese, grated

DIRECTIONS

Preheat oven to 350°F (180°C, Gas Mark 4).

In large saucepan or soup pot, boil potatoes and rutabaga in salted water until very tender 40-45 minutes. Drain and mash well. Stir in milk and 2 tablespoons butter.

In another large saucepan boil cabbage for 5 minutes, drain well and stir into the mash.

Sauté onion in remaining 2 tablespoons butter until tender. Stir into mash mixture and season with salt and pepper.

Turn into a greased casserole and sprinkle with cheese. Bake until cheese bubbles, 20-30 minutes.

NOTES: Add any leftover vegetables you like. Rumbledethumps isn't so much a recipe as a suggestion for a type of dish: a vegetable-mash bake. It's good for brunch topped with an egg.

Rumbledethumps is an easy dish to do in stages. Mix up the mash and cabage ahead; the day you want to serve it, top with cheese and bake.

As written here, it's enough Rumbledethumps to serve 8-10.

Adapted from recipe at BBC Food Recipes[1].

---

1. https://www.bbc.com/food/recipes/rumbledethumps_87486

CAULIFLOWER CHEESE AND WHISKY

Never has cauliflower been so soused. Though there does seem to be rather a lot of various types of alcohol in this cookbook, the alcohol cooks out and leaves behind unique flavor. That's certainly true in this vegetable side dish.

INGREDIENTS

One medium cauliflower

6 ounces (170g) mushrooms, finely chopped

Half of a green pepper, finely chopped

1¼ cups (300ml) whipping cream (double cream)

1 cup (113g) sharp Cheddar cheese, grated

6 tablespoons (90ml) whisky

1 tablespoon (12g) fine oatmeal (see *NOTES*)

¼ teaspoon nutmeg

Salt and pepper

½ cup (67g) choice of unsalted nuts, chopped

DIRECTIONS

Preheat oven to 350°F (180°C, Gas Mark 4).

Cut off cauliflower stalks and cook florets in hot water for five minutes. Drain and put in a bowl.

Mix in mushrooms and green peppers. Turn into an ovenproof dish.

In a saucepan, heat cream over medium heat but do not boil. Add cheese, stirring frequently. When cheese is melted, remove from heat and stir in whisky. Add oatmeal, a little at a time, stirring constantly. Add salt, pepper, and nutmeg to taste. Pour over cauliflower and sprinkle chopped nuts on top.

Bake 45-55 minutes. Let stand 10 minutes and serve.

NOTES: Guessing at what "fine oatmeal" is, I ground 1 tablespoon steel cut oats in a coffee grinder. You could also try processing rolled oats in the small bowl of your food processor.

For the 1¼ cups whipping cream I used 1 cup whipping cream and ¼ cup low-fat buttermilk not because I tried to cut down on the calories but because that's what I had. It worked fine.

Serve with rice or potatoes.

A word about whisky: The Scotch determines the flavor of this dish, so if you're not familiar with the spirit, in general, the lighter the amber color of the liquor, the more subtle the flavor. I used a dark smoky blended Scotch, and the flavor of the cheese sauce was decidedly not subtle. I was a little concerned as the cooking progressed, boozy odors drifting from the oven, but it turned out great.

And another word about whisky: It's "whisky" for the spirit made in Scotland, and it's "whiskey" for the different spirit made in the US (usually bourbon). Use the terms whisky and Scotch interchangeably to clarify that it's Scotch from Scotland.

Adapted from recipe at Rampant Scotland[1].

---

http://www.rampantscotland.com/recipes/blrecipe_cauliflower.htm

CRUSTY NO-KNEAD BREAD

Baked in a Dutch oven at high heat, this bread is as easy as it is scrumptiou Mix up the dough the evening before and forget about it until the next a ternoon, and you've got fresh bread for dinner.

In *Love Inherited*, China stops by Granny Nan's for a bite of lunch. The brea she slices up to go with their cheese and pickle is browned to perfection, with crackly crust and a moist crumb.

INGREDIENTS

3 cups (375g) unbleached all-purpose (plain) flour

¼ teaspoon instant yeast

1¼ teaspoons (7g) salt

1½ cups plus 2 tablespoons (384ml) water

DIRECTIONS

In a large bowl combine flour, yeast, and salt.

Add water and stir until blended. Dough will be very sticky.

Cover bowl with plastic wrap and let rest 12-18 hours at room temperatur Dough is ready when bubbly all over the surface.

Line a clean bowl or proofing basket with parchment paper (a bowl rough the size of your Dutch oven). Trim paper. You will be lifting the dough out of th bowl in the paper, so leave enough to grab the paper and plop the dough into very hot Dutch oven.

Lightly flour work surface and turn dough onto it. Sprinkle dough and you fingers with flour and gently stretch and fold dough over on itself in thirds. D this stretch and fold two or three times in opposite directions. Dough is ve sticky and is supposed to be.

Flour your hands and shape dough into a ball by cupping your hands aroun the dough and gently pulling toward you. Place dough into parchment-line bowl, seam side down. Cover with a cotton tea towel and let rise about 2 hour

Dough should double in volume and not spring back much when poked with a finger.

Place 3- or 5-quart enamel or cast iron covered Dutch oven in oven while oven preheats. (I've used both sizes for this recipe. The loaf comes out a little flatter in the larger pot.) At least a half-hour before dough is ready, preheat oven to 500°F (260°C, Gas Mark 10). Then turn temperature down to 450°F (230°C, Gas Mark 8). When dough is ready, lift out with the paper and set on counter, dust with flour if desired, and slash top of dough with sharp, preferably serrated, knife or bread lame. This allows the loaf to bloom quickly in the high heat.

Remove pot from oven and *carefully* lift dough by the paper and plop into the pot, parchment paper and all. Shake the pot gently if the dough needs settling, but it should straighten out as it bakes.

Cover with lid and bake 30 minutes. Remove lid and bake another 20 minutes until loaf is browned to perfection (try not to open the oven). Cool on a rack.

NOTES: Add whatever you like: seeds, herbs, cracked pepper.

I whisk dry ingredients together in the bowl of a stand mixer, then mix in water using the dough hook. I transfer the dough to a large crockery bowl because I like homemade bread rising in an earthy bowl.

I use the parchment paper method for the second rising because I just can't handle the sticky dough.

When transferring the dough to the Dutch oven, don't have too much paper hanging over the top, and don't stuff too much paper over the dough in the pot, but do get the lid on tight. Using paper in the baking, you might get some wonky dents in the bread, but that's okay.

Baking with high heat can be a little tricky. When I first made this recipe, the bread burned on the bottom. Use a baking stone, or fold several layers of aluminum foil into a square and place under the pot.

If you use a cooking thermometer to test for done, the bread's internal temp should be 180-200°F (82-93°C).

Adapted from recipe by Jim Lahey.

OATCAKES

Traditional Scottish Oatcakes are made with no sugar and no flour. Not a cake at all but more like a cracker, oatcakes are perfect with jam, butter, or cheese, or plain with soup.

After a few floundering, but tasty, attempts at coming up with an oatcake I liked, I hit on these Goldilocks oatcakes: *just right*. I want a dough that's not too dry to roll out, and I want an oatcake that won't crumble at the sight of a butter knife, yet has a nice oaty taste.

To get there, I finally gave up on trying to interpret British oatcake recipes for the US kitchen (what's "medium oats"?), and I turned to Bob Moore of Bob's Red Mill. I figured he must know oats since he won the Golden Spurtle award in 2016. In Bob's Favorite Scottish Oatcakes recipe, the main ingredient is Bob's Red Mill Scottish Oatmeal. American cooks, I recommend using this product to take the guesswork out of the oats issue.

UK cooks, I didn't convert this recipe. Since you know the British Secret Language of Oats, you can make your granny's oatcake recipe—or just go out and buy a box of excellent oatcakes.

INGREDIENTS

1½ cups Bob's Red Mill Scottish Oatmeal

½ cup whole wheat pastry flour

¾ teaspoon granulated sugar

¼ teaspoon salt

¼ teaspoon baking powder

¼ cup unsalted butter, melted

¼-⅓ cup hot water

DIRECTIONS

Preheat oven to 375°F.

Place all dry ingredients in a bowl and mix thoroughly.

Add melted butter and stir.

Add water a little at a time. Stir in with a fork (like pastry dough) until just moistened. Don't overwork.

Using your hands, form dough into a ball.

Sprinkle pastry cloth or work surface with a couple tablespoons of the whole wheat pastry flour and turn dough out onto it. Use a surface that won't get damaged with a cookie cutter or knife. I use a pastry cloth on a frame.

Flatten dough slightly and roll out to ¼ inch thick.

Using a 2- or 3-inch cookie or biscuit cutter, cut into rounds. Gather scraps and roll out again until all the dough is used up. Alternatively, with a knife, cut dough into squares.

Transfer to a parchment-lined baking sheet and place rounds slightly apart.

Bake 20-30 minutes or until golden brown. If oatcakes aren't slightly golden round the edges, they're not done.

Cool on a rack and store in airtight container.

Adapted from recipe at Bob's Red Mill[1].

https://www.bobsredmill.com/recipes/how-to-make/bobs-favorite-scottish-oatcakes/

SCONES

Romancing the scone—the pursuit of the perfect scone. I like mine as drop scone clouds: golden on the outside and moist and tender on the inside. Any flavor will do, but in my opinion, they're best with oats. The Scots would probably agree since they seem to add oats to everything.

Sylvie always has scones made and ready to serve anyone who stops by Crag gan Mhor for a cuppa—like Duncan Sinclair, the handsome laird next door.

INGREDIENTS—makes about 12 drop scones

1½ cups (188g) all-purpose (plain) flour

2 cups (200g) rolled oats (or substitute 1 cup of oats with 1 cup oat bran for smoother texture)

¼ cup (56g) granulated (caster) sugar

4 teaspoons (16g) baking powder

½ teaspoon salt

½ cup (71g) currants or dried fruit of choice

1 egg, beaten, room temperature

½ cup (113g) unsalted butter, melted

⅓ cup (78ml) milk, room temperature (increase milk to ½ cup [118ml] making drop scones)

DIRECTIONS

Preheat oven to 425°F (220°C, Gas Mark 7) for at least 15-20 minutes.

Combine flour, oats, sugar, baking powder, salt, and dried fruit in large bowl and mix well.

Beat egg until frothy. Mix in melted butter and milk (remember to increase milk if making drop scones).

Make a well in flour mixture and pour egg mixture into well.

Stir into soft dough until just combined. Do not beat smooth.

Either divide dough and pat into two 6- to 7-inch rounds on a lightly floured surface, scoring tops into 8 wedges, or drop even dollops onto greased or parchment-lined baking sheet. Flatten drop scones slightly.

Bake 15 minutes until risen and golden brown. Ovens vary in actual temperature, and baking time may need to be increased to 20-25 minutes.

Serve warm with butter and jam—and of course, tea.

NOTES: If making wedge scones, you may need to wet knife blade and slice edges apart, separating slightly to get edges done.

Adapted from recipe at Genius Kitchen[1].

SCOTTISH SHORTBREAD

The perfect bit of something to go along with your tea or coffee, this traditional Scottish Shortbread isn't too sweet but sweet enough. Sure, you can buy shortbread off the grocery shelf—look for the red tartan box—but there's something satisfying about making your own.

Sylvie has China mixing up shortbread, a Scottish holiday staple, in preparation for the *Hogmanay party at Craggan Mhor.

INGREDIENTS—makes about 15 rounds

1⅓ cups (166g) all-purpose (plain) flour

¼ cup (28g) cornstarch (cornflour)

½ cup (113g) unsalted butter, softened

¼ cup (56g) granulated (caster) sugar

optional—1-2 teaspoons flavored extract or grated orange or lemon zest

3-4 tablespoons cold water (including any extract added)

DIRECTIONS

Preheat oven to 325°F (165°C, Gas Mark 3).

Sift (sieve) flour and cornstarch together into a bowl and set aside.

Using a stand mixer with paddle attachment, mix butter and sugar together until creamy. Add flavored extract or zest if desired.

Add flour to butter and mix until mixture resembles coarse crumbs. (Treat this dough just like a pie crust.) Add water, a little at a time, until dough starts to come together. Do not overwork or knead.

Pat dough into a ball and chill 10 minutes.

Liberally dust work surface with flour and turn dough out onto work surface. Dust top of dough and pat a little flatter. Or place dough between sheets of plastic wrap or parchment paper. Roll dough out to ¼ to ½ inch thick.

Prick dough all over with a fork and cut into rounds. Or cut into 1x3 inch fingers. Keep gathering the scraps and reshaping until all dough is used up.

Place shortbread cookies onto a parchment-lined baking tray. Bake for 25-45 minutes or until done to a pale brown around the edges. Turn tray in oven halfway through baking.

Shake a little sugar on top immediately after removing from oven. Cool thoroughly on a rack before storing in an airtight container.

NOTES: Make the recipe your own; add any extract or citrus zest; substitute a bit of cornmeal or rice flour for the flour; substitute brown sugar for some of the sugar.

For a delicate flavor, try lavender. Place the buds of two lavender flowers (English lavender is reported to be the sweetest) or ¾-1 teaspoon dried lavender in a coffee grinder with 1-2 tablespoons of the sugar from the recipe. Grind together until fine, breaking apart the buds and releasing the essential oils. Culinary grade lavender is recommended.

You'll notice there's quite a range for baking time. Baking time will vary depending on your preference for the thickness and desired crispness of the cookie. Some recipes call for an oven temperature of 350°F, but most heat to 325°F, so that's what I stuck with—and I checked for doneness and added time as necessary. The cookies need to bake long enough to dry out and crisp a bit. Better to bake them a little longer and have browned edges than be underdone.

The texture and taste of this recipe is a little different from the shortbread I'm familiar with, having eaten only the commercial variety. It's not as grainy, not as sweet, and, unflavored, the cornstarch taste comes through just a tad. I'm now a fan of lavender flavor. And I'll be making my own shortbread from now on.

*Hogmanay (HOG-ma-NAY) is the Scottish New Year's Eve celebration. A two- to three-day party with numerous, sometimes regional, traditions, Hogmanay goes back a long way. This may be in part because the celebration of Christmas was discouraged by the Church of Scotland for 400 years. Christmas only became a public holiday in 1958.

Adapted from recipe at Rampant Scotland[1].

---

1.   http://www.rampantscotland.com/recipes/blrecipe_shortbread.htm

TIPSY LAIRD

Tipsy Laird is often served as the dessert course at a *Burn's Night Supper or on Hogmanay. This Scottish version of the English Trifle is both a visual treat and easy to make.

Make Tipsy Laird in one large glass trifle bowl to show off the pretty layers or divided into individual glass compote dishes.

INGREDIENTS

10 ounces (285g) pound cake, halved, cut into thick slices

10 ounces (285g) fresh raspberries

6 tablespoons (90ml) Scotch (whisky) or Drambuie (juice for a nonalcoholic version)

2 cups (472ml) thick custard sauce

2 cups (472ml) whipping cream (double cream), softly whipped

Handful toasted slivered (flaked) almonds

optional—grated chocolate over the top

DIRECTIONS

Arrange cake slices in bottom of the dish.

Layer raspberries, reserving a few to decorate the top.

Drizzle liquor or juice over raspberries.

Spoon custard over in thick layer.

Spoon whipped cream over.

Decorate the top with a few raspberries and toasted slivered almonds.

NOTES: I recommend Bird's Custard Powder. It's a great egg-free custard shortcut that has been in UK cooks' pantries since 1844. But the trick to getting the custard thick enough is to add seriously heaping tablespoons (US) of the powder. And, Americans, remember to adjust the milk; the UK pint is 20 ounces. Use a twig whisk to prevent lumps.

Scotch is what makes this dessert Scottish. But if you're not a fan of Scotch, I recommend you go with Drambuie, a sweet Scotch-based liqueur, and you can still call it Scottish. Of course, a trifle by any name, or with any flavored liquid soaking into the cake and raspberries, will taste as sweet.

Don't make the trifle too far ahead.

*What's a Burn's Night Supper? The Scots revere Robert Burns, and the 25th of January, the poet's birthday, is a night of revelry and ritual like only the Scots can do; it involves bagpipes, haggis, and whisky. There's quite the Burn's Night Supper in *Love Inherited*.

Adapted from recipe at The Spruce Eats[1].

MRS. PORTER'S CHEESECAKE

W hat's Scottish about this no-bake, no-eggs cheesecake? It's the McVitie's Digestive Biscuit crust.

Nothing other than McVitie's Digestives will do for the crust, in my opinion. McVitie's Digestives were created in 1892 by a genius employee of the Edinburgh biscuit company, McVitie & Price, and they were quickly embraced by the whole of the UK. The plain, graham-flavored cookie was called Digestive due to the high baking soda content which was thought to aid digestion. They sure make my tummy happy.

But why is this recipe called Mrs. Porter's Cheesecake? Because Mrs. Porter was my friend Sue's mother; Mrs. Porter handed down this recipe to Sue, and Sue handed it to me. It's my hands down favorite cheesecake.

The connection with *Love Inherited* is that Mrs. Porter had a West Highland White Terrier named Andy. A jaunty, likable little fellow, Andy found his way into *Love Inherited* when Sylvie needed a dog: obedient when he wants to be, quick to give chase, and sweet.

CRUST INGREDIENTS

6 crushed McVitie's Digestive Biscuits

4 tablespoons (56g) butter

3 tablespoons (38g) brown (demerara) sugar

CRUST DIRECTIONS

Crush biscuits (see *NOTES*) and place in mixing bowl.

Melt butter and sugar together.

Add butter to crushed biscuits and mix.

Flatten crust on bottom of 7-inch glass pie plate. Lightly press using the bottom of a glass, metal measuring cup, or a spoon.

Chill 1-2 hours.

FILLING INGREDIENTS

8 ounces (225g) cream cheese
6 tablespoons (84g) granulated (caster) sugar
Juice of 1 lemon or 3 tablespoons lemon juice concentrate
½ cup plus 2 tablespoons (147ml) whipping cream (double cream)

FILLING DIRECTIONS

Mix cream cheese and sugar, blending thoroughly until creamy.
Add lemon juice, beat smooth.
In separate bowl, whip cream until thick using electric hand mixer.
Fold whipped cream into cheese mixture.
Spoon on top of biscuit crust. Smooth and level the surface.
Chill.
Serve topped with whatever you like: grated dark chocolate, toasted coconut, fresh fruit.

NOTES: Place the biscuits in a zip plastic bag and roll into fine crumbs with a rolling pin.
I use a stand mixer with paddle attachment to beat the filling smooth.
Make this cheesecake a day or two ahead for the flavors to fully meld.

STICKY TOFFEE PUDDING

The British refer to all desserts as pudding. So Sticky Toffee Pudding isn'
pudding in American-speak, but rather, it's a date cake swimming i
caramel goo.

Sticky Toffee Pudding is a modern concoction. It's unclear who's really th
originator, but it is clear that when the dessert hit the restaurant scene in th
north of England in the 1970s, it took off in popularity, spreading throughou
the UK.

I first tasted Sticky Toffee Pudding in Invergarry, Scotland, and it was love a
first bite. I had to include it in *Love Inherited*. China discovers Sticky Pud
ding at the quirky Wildcat Cafe, and she too is smitten.

Don't count the calories, just enjoy.

INGREDIENTS

Cake

1¼ cups (224g) pitted dates, finely chopped

1 cup (236ml) boiling water

2 tablespoons instant coffee granules, or 2 teaspoons espresso coffee powde

1 teaspoon (6g) baking soda (bicarbonate of soda)

1 teaspoon pure vanilla extract

1¾ cups (219g) all-purpose (plain) flour

½ teaspoon (2g) baking powder

½ cup (113g) unsalted butter, room temperature

1 cup (213g) packed brown (demerara) sugar, light or dark

4 large eggs, room temperature

Sauce

2 cups (472ml) whipping cream (double cream)

1 cup (220g) packed dark brown (demerara) sugar

¼ cup (56g) unsalted butter

optional—1 tablespoon Drambuie

DIRECTIONS

Cake

Place chopped dates in small bowl. Pour boiling water over dates. Add coffee granules, baking soda, and vanilla. Stir to dissolve. Let cool about an hour.

Preheat oven to 350°F (180°C, Gas Mark 4).

Butter pan 8x8x2 inches (20x20x5 cm).

Mix flour and baking powder and set aside.

Using electric mixer, beat butter and sugar in large bowl. Scrape sides of bowl often during mixing process.

Add 2 eggs, one at a time, beating well after each. Add half of flour and beat to blend. Add remaining 2 eggs, one at a time. Add remaining flour and beat until blended.

Fold date mixture into batter with a spoon and mix well.

Pour batter into prepared pan. Level batter.

Bake 50 minutes to 1 hour until tester inserted into center comes out clean.

Let cake cool in pan. Run a knife around the sides to loosen. Poke holes all over cake with a skewer.

Sauce

Let the cake cool before starting the sauce.

In medium saucepan, bring cream, brown sugar, and butter to a gentle boil over medium-high heat, stirring frequently.

Reduce heat and simmer sauce, stirring occasionally, about 15 minutes. Sauce should reduce and thicken a little.

Remove from heat. Add optional Drambuie. Let cool a few minutes.

Pour *half* of warm (not hot) sauce over level cake (see *NOTES*). Cool to room temperature, then refrigerate. Do not cover. In about an hour, when sauce is firm, cover pan with plastic wrap and refrigerate if not serving immediately.

Reserve remainder of sauce.

To serve, cut servings and heat in microwave until caramel melts. Warm reserved sticky toffee sauce and pour it on. Top with whipped cream or vanilla ice cream.

NOTES: After the cake cools, you may need to carefully remove it from the pan and get it level by slicing off the high spot on the top, otherwise, when you pour on the sauce you'll get a puddle of sauce around the edges with an island mound of cake in the middle.

That said, I couldn't safely get the cake out of the pan to level it. I settled for running a long bread knife flat across the top edge of the pan, slicing off the cake dome. Then I poked lots of holes in the cake to let in the caramel.

Adapted from recipe at Christina's Cucina[1].

1.   https://www.christinascucina.com/sticky-toffee-pudding-heaven-on-plate/

ATHOLL BROSE

A Scottish drink, Atholl Brose is traditionally served at Hogmanay. But since it contains whisky, I doubt very much that its consumption is limited to ne evening a year.

The name derives from *brose*, a Scots term for uncooked, steeped oat-eal—and the Earl of Atholl, the legendary creator of the beverage.

The story goes—in 1475 the Earl of Atholl was called upon by King James I of Scotland to quell a rebellion of Highlanders led by the Earl of Ross. On a connaissance mission, Atholl's men observed the Highlanders drinking from a articular well. Inspiration struck the Earl, and he decided to spike the well with ats, honey, and whisky. The Highlanders discovered the tainted well and drank eir fill, making the ensuing battle much shorter, the outcome going in favor of e Earl of Atholl.

Serving Atholl Brose as a military strategy is questionable, but I can attest at it's a fine way to ring in the new year—with friends beside a cozy fire, the soft ystal *tink* of glasses met in a toast.

INGREDIENTS

½ cup oats, rolled or steel cut (pinhead) (50g/100g)

1½ cups (354ml) water

1 tablespoon honey

1 cup (236ml) Scotch blend, or amount equal to oat water

Whipping cream (double cream) to taste

DIRECTIONS

Steep the water and oats for 24 hours.

Strain off the oats, squeezing out as much liquid as you can. (see *NOTES*)

Add the honey. Tradition says to stir with a silver spoon.

Add the Scotch and stir.

Pour into a clean bottle and refrigerate two or three days for the flavors to meld.

At serving, add whipping cream to taste and stir.

NOTES: If you want the oat water milkier, use rolled oats.

To strain the oats, I use an old linen tea towel lining a sieve. Discard the oat or eat for breakfast.

There's also a dessert version of Atholl Brose with whipped cream and raspberries. Replace the whipped cream with crowdie, and you've got Cranachan. But that's for another cookbook.

Slàinte!

Adapted from recipe at Christina's Cucina[1].

---

1.   https://www.christinascucina.com/atholl-brose-with-and-without-cream/

A NOTE TO READERS

Thank you for taking the time to read *A Wee Scottish Cookbook*—and maybe cooking up a few of the recipes. I had a lot of fun writing it and taste-testing everything at least once. I hope you enjoyed *A Wee Scottish Cookbook*.

If you'd post a review on Amazon, I'd really appreciate it.

If you'd like to communicate directly with me, send an email through my website: CristineEastin.com[1].

ABOUT THE AUTHOR

CRISTINE EASTIN writes contemporary women's fiction spiced with romance, threaded with life's heartaches, and enriched with faith and hope.

Cris grew up in Minnesota where life centered on family and friends, outdoor activities, pets, music, and reading. She also wrote short stories and terrible poetry. Then the fun writing stopped and she attended the university. She earned a doctorate in counseling from the University of Wisconsin-Madison.

A psychotherapist for over thirty years, Cris has a passion for encouraging people. She tells patients who feel dried up inside, "You can't pour from an empty pitcher." Writing for fun again, Cris hopes her fiction not only entertains but pours into readers' deepest needs.

Cris and her husband live in Wisconsin, not too far from the grandkids.

She's a member of American Christian Fiction Writers (ACFW).

Visit Cris at her website: CristineEastin.com[1].

---

1.   http://www.cristineeastin.com

ALSO BY
CRISTINE EASTIN

LOVE INHERITED

Love is a disaster for China MacLeish.

Her fiancé walks out. She hasn't heard from her mother in two years. She's creeping up on middle age. And she's fuming.

Then her life gets weird.

A letter arrives informing her she has inherited an estate in the Highlands of Scotland from an unknown uncle. But she must live in the manor for one year before the property—and a lot of money—is hers. Hopping mad about disrupting her career, she leaves Chicago and friends behind to try to survive in seldom-sunny Scotland, only to discover secrets her mother kept from her—family secrets.

But when China meets her neighbor Duncan Sinclair, Laird of Fionnloch, she's torn apart. She doesn't know whether he's a friend, a man with too much emotional baggage, or a Highland dream come true.

Could her life and love get any more complicated and confusing?

PRAISE FOR *Love Inherited*:

"She has to travel miles to find home, mingle with strangers to know who she is, and face past heartaches to learn love."

"It is a rare book that can sweep me away like this one did....a Scottish stay-cation that felt so real, I walked away feeling happy and relaxed..."

"Truly, this book will have you dreaming in plaid..."

FIFTY DAYS TO SUNRISE

Her life is a love story, but then...What's a woman to do when her husband dies three thousand miles from home? Scream, cry—or run?

It's a year and a half after her husband's death. Fifty-three years old and alone, Lissa Maguire's seething with grief. She has to cope but makes a self-destructive mess of it.

Lissa's parents ask her to spend the summer in small-town Gifford, Minnesota, helping them move to an apartment. Cleaning out the attic of her childhood home, Lissa discovers her old diaries, and her potholed road to healing begins.

But when an old friend turns up, she's confused...and surprised.

PRAISE FOR *Fifty Days to Sunrise:*

"Told with a rare authenticity and grace, *Fifty Days to Sunrise* is much more than a story but a hallowed place with people who are so finely crafted and multi-layered they feel more like family and friends. Cristine Eastin has given us an honest, memorable look at grief, love, healing, and home. Readers will want more of these characters and this author!"—Laura Frantz, author of *A Moonbow Night*

"I sincerely felt like I was right there, in the midst of the family...I found myself crying, laughing, and struggling along with Lissa, her parents, siblings, and friends."

"Nice to read a faith-based book that holds your attention and makes you feel good."

BOOKS BY CRISTINE EASTIN are available on Amazon in print and ebook editions.